The Invisible Child
WAR'S UNSPEAKABLE BARGAIN

*A world that has made itself good for a child
is a good world.*

Sebastian Barry

The Invisible Child
WAR'S UNSPEAKABLE BARGAIN

To the children killed, wounded, traumatized, displaced, orphaned in Russia's War on Ukraine

The Invisible Child
WAR'S UNSPEAKABLE BARGAIN

Contents

Foreword 1

A Story
First Telling 5
Second Telling 7
Third Telling 11

A Promise 15

A Fourth Telling 19

Thank You 22

Credits 23

Fields of Peace 27

The Invisible Child
WAR'S UNSPEAKABLE BARGAIN

Copyright © 2022 / All Rights Reserved
Charles P. Busch / Fields of Peace

All rights reserved. No part of this book may be reproduced or transmitted in any form or by any means, electronic or mechanical, including photocopying, recording or by any information storage and retrieval system, without written permission of the publisher, except for inclusion of brief quotations in a review.

ISBN: 978-1-7371828-2-5

Fields of Peace
3355 Otter Crest Loop
Depoe Bay, Oregon 97341
USA

fieldsofpeace.org

Cover Photograph
michaelnye.org

Layout & Design
timmyroland.com

The Invisible Child
WAR'S UNSPEAKABLE BARGAIN

Charles P. Busch

Fields of Peace

The Invisible Child
WAR'S UNSPEAKABLE BARGAIN

Foreword

In 1991, my friend Michael Nye traveled to Northern Iraq to be a witness to the suffering of the Kurdish people who had become refugees in their own land. It was a time of war. The Kurds, after decades of harsh rule by the Iraqi government, had rebelled and were demanding self rule and independence. Iraqi soldiers, in village after village, were rounding up civilians and executing them. More than 400,000 Kurds fled their homes.

Hitching rides on trucks and helicopters, and on foot, Michael found his way to refugee encampments in the mountains near the Turkish border. There he was welcomed. He was a stranger who cared and risked to be with them. Families invited him into their tents, offering self-rolled cigarettes, tea hot from a campfire, and stories of the war that chased them there. One father, eyes down, speaking slowly, told him: "Ten days ago Iraqi soldiers entered our village. They ordered us to stand outside our house. While we watched, a soldier shot and killed my youngest. She was seven. The soldier then demanded I pay him for the bullet that killed her."

"Their stories made me cry," Michael said. "They would make anyone cry."

The photograph of a Kurdish girl on the cover of this booklet was taken by Michael during his time among the refugees. To me, she is *The Invisible Child*, a haunting image to remind us of the children killed in war. Find a place for her on your desk or a shelf where you can see her, keep company with her. May she speak to you, as she does to me, of our first duty as adults: To make a world that is good for children.

Charles P. Busch
Fields of Peace

A Story

The Invisible Child
WAR'S UNSPEAKABLE BARGAIN

First Telling

World War One was my grandparents' war. They lived in a small town in Nebraska and ran a grocery and dry goods store. They sent the hometown boys, mostly farm boys, off with a parade. They prayed for them, bought war bonds, tried to believe it was "the war to end all wars."

In that war, it was mostly soldiers who died. They fought in farm fields—wheat, flax, grazing fields—that became battle fields. Civilian casualties were unintended. For every nine combatants killed, one civilian was killed. A ratio of **9 to 1**.

In the town park a memorial was put up to honor our boys who didn't come back. A metal plaque on an obelisk listed the names, about a dozen. As a boy playing in the park I would sometimes go over and read the names, moving my fingers over the raised letters. Privates and corporals with last names I knew. The dates made the subtraction easy. Most were 18 or 19. One was 16. I'd wonder if there was a war waiting for me when I finished school.

~

The Story is from *The Brothers Karamazov* by Fyodor Dostoyevsky. I keep it nearby in the bookcase next to my desk. I like to take it down and open to one of the pages with a turned down corner and read what's there. On page 245, there's a conversation between two brothers, Ivan and Aloysha. They are in the parlor of their father's house.

It is late at night and they are alone.

Ivan, the oldest of four brothers, has come home for a visit. He lives far off in the big city of Moscow. He is a philosopher and a cynic, maybe an atheist. Aloysha is the youngest of the brothers. He is pure in heart and a novice in a monastery. He adores his oldest brother, and looks up to him.

Their conversation takes them to the subject of human suffering—poverty, hunger, injustice, war—and what can be done about it. Ivan challenges Aloysha with a hypothetical bargain. He says:

> Imagine you have the power to restructure the world. Make it a world in which everyone has everything they need to be happy---food, home, work, and peace, a lasting peace. But for all this to happen, there is a price. A single, one-time price: you must torture to death one tiny child. A perfect world for the price of one nameless child. Would you consent to that bargain?

No, Aloysha answers, *I would not consent.*

Second Telling

World War Two was my parent's war. They ran the weekly newspaper in our Nebraska town. With other town folk and the high school band, they stood on the station platform and waved as the Union Pacific train took the boys off to Omaha and on to war. They planted victory gardens and led scrap-metal drives, and sent packages with cigarettes and baked goods to overseas addresses. Each morning my father put up the flag in front of our house.

In their war, the ratio of combatant deaths to civilian deaths had changed dramatically. It was no longer 9 to 1, but **1 to 1**. For every combatant killed, one civilian was killed. Airplanes and the bombing of cities account for the change. London. Dresden, Tokyo. Hiroshima. In all, over six years, about 70 million people died in that war. About 1,465 every hour. It has been called "the Good War."

~

The Story is from "The Ones Who Walk Away from Omelas," by Ursula K. Le Guin. I came across a magazine article that described the story's plot. It sounded a lot like Ivan's challenge to Aloysha, so I found a copy. The word "Omelas" in the title is "Salem" spelled backwards with the exclamation "O" in front. Salem means peace. Le Guin writes:

In a basement under one of the beautiful public buildings of Omelas, or perhaps in the cellar of one of its spacious private homes, there is a room. It has one locked door, and no window. A little light seeps in . . . secondhand from a cobwebbed window somewhere across the cellar. In one corner of the little room a couple of mops, with stiff, clotted, foul-smelling heads, stand near a rusty bucket. The floor is dirt, a little damp to the touch... The room is about three paces long and two wide: a mere broom closet or disused tool room.

In the room a child is sitting. It could be a boy or a girl. It looks about six but actually is nearly ten. It is feeble-minded. Perhaps it was born defective, or perhaps it has become imbecile through fear, malnutrition, and neglect. It picks its nose and occasionally fumbles vaguely with its toes or genitals, as it sits hunched in the corner farthest from the bucket and the two mops. It is afraid of the mops. It finds them horrible.

The door is always locked; and nobody ever comes, except that sometimes—the child has no understanding of time or interval—sometimes the door rattles terribly and opens, and a person, or several people, are there. One of them may come in and kick the child to make it stand up. The others never come close, but peer in at it with frightened, disgusted eyes. The food bowl and the water jug are hastily filled, the door is locked, the eyes disappear. The people at the door never say anything, but the child, who has not always lived in the tool room, and can remember sunlight and its mother's voice, sometimes speaks. "I will be good," it says. "Please let me out. I will be good!" They never answer. The child used to scream for help at night, and cry a good deal, but now it only makes a kind of whining.

"eh-has, e-has," and it speaks less and less often. It is so thin there are no calves to its legs; its belly protrudes; it lives on a half-bowl of corn meal and grease a day. It is naked. Its buttocks and thighs are a mass of festered sores, as it sits in its own excrement continually.

They all know it is there, all the people of Omelas. Some of them have come to see it, others are content merely to know it is there. They all know that it has to be there. Some of them understand why, and some do not, but they all understand that their happiness, the beauty of their city, the tenderness of their friendships, the health of their children, the wisdom of their scholars, the skill of their makers, even the abundance of their harvest and the kindly weather of their skies, depend wholly on this child's abominable misery.

Le Guin offers this story as a myth. We are not told what requires the sacrifice of the child, or how the misery of one provides the happiness for so many. But the bargain is clear and strict. If even one kind word were spoken to the child, the charmed life of the city would fall apart. The citizens there are not barbarians, nor do they lack sophistication or compassion. They simply accept that life involves injustice, and assume their privilege. There are exceptions, especially among the young. But they are few. They are the ones who walk away from Omelas.

The Invisible Child
WAR'S UNSPEAKABLE BARGAIN

Third Telling

The Vietnam War was my war. I was in the Marine Corps Reserves for eight years of it. I lived in a south Texas city and worked for a large international corporation. One weekend a month and two weeks each summer, I put on fatigues and trained with my Reserve Unit. I wasn't eager to go to Vietnam, but willing.

During those years, each evening I watched CBS news with Walter Cronkite. I saw the flag-draped coffins lined up on airport runways. I saw girls put long-stemmed flowers in the barrels of soldier's rifles. I read the Pentagon Papers in the *New York Times*, and still remember the photograph on the cover of *Time* of a Vietnamese girl running naked down a street, fleeing fire.

I got lucky, our Reserve Unit wasn't called up. When my Honorable Discharge came, I celebrated by going to New York City to visit friends. One morning, stepping out to buy a paper, I saw that Broadway was lined with people. And coming up the street, a stream of people, smiling, waving, holding signs and banners, "Make love not war." "Give peace a chance." A parade of young and old. Moms and dads pushing strollers. Children skipping, waving little flags. I waved back. The stream kept coming. "Hey, Hey LBJ, how many kids did you kill today?" I stepped off the curb and walked with them. Somebody handed me a sign, "Imagine Peace." We walked all the way up to Columbia University, about 50 blocks.

On the subway back, I felt happy, light as a balloon. I liked that it was my feet, not my head, that had known what to do.

In the decades since that War, other U.S. wars and military actions have followed. It's a long list: Iran, El Salvador, Libya, Lebanon, Granada, Chad, Persian Gulf, Honduras, Panama, Columbia, Philippines, Liberia, Kuwait, Iraq, Bosnia and Herzegovina, Somalia, Haiti, Sudan, Serbia, Afghanistan, Yemen, Iraq, Cameroon, Pakistan, Syria.

Serial wars became perpetual war. And the ratio of combatant deaths to civilian deaths again changed dramatically: **1 to 9**. For every 1 combatant killed, 9 civilians are killed, the majority of them children. Modern war has become the killing of children.

The logic hit me:

> *If the killing of a child is an absolute wrong,*
> *If war has become the killing of children,*
> *Then I cannot be a part of any war, no matter how lofty the reason.*

Feeling the need to do something, I met with friends and we started *Fields of Peace*, a small nonprofit with a big Mission: *to stop the killing of children in wars*. Like Dostoyevsky and Le Guin, we told a story about *The Invisible Child*.

~

The story is from Fields of Peace. *Imagine yourself on an airport runway. It is early morning, barely light. You are wearing a pilot's jumpsuit, and behind you is a huge stealth bomber, black as a bat. Standing with you is a five-year-old girl in a pink party dress. The two of you are alone. You don't know her and she doesn't know you.*

But she is looking up at you and she is smiling. Her face has a copper glow, and she is beautiful, utterly beautiful.

Inside your pocket is a cigarette lighter. Before you fly the plane, you've been ordered to do up close what you will do later in the day to other children from 30 thousand feet. You are to set her dress on fire, to set her on fire. You've been told the reason. It's a lofty one.

You kneel, and look up. The girl is curious, still smiling. You take out the lighter. She has no idea. It helps you not to know her name.

But you cannot do it. Of course you can't.

The Invisible Child
WAR'S UNSPEAKABLE BARGAIN

A Promise

The next war will be my son Gabriel's war, but it need not happen. War is no more inevitable than a single harsh word, shove, or moment of indifference to suffering of another. Always there is a choice. You and I can say "no" to the next war, "no" to the killing of children. And we can begin by doing something obvious and immediate: make *A Promise to Our Children*. This *Promise*:

> *I will not be a part of the killing*
> *of any child,*
> *no matter how lofty the reason.*
> *Not my neighbor's child. Not my child.*
> *Not the enemy's child.*
> *Not by bomb. Not by bullet.*
> *Not by looking the other way.*
> *I will be the power that is peace.*

This handful of words may seem slight, no more than a wish, set against the machinery of war—its armies, its industry, its propaganda. But words hold the power of creation. Nothing new begins without them. Said out loud—like a prayer, psalm, pledge—they travel *Out*. And when the moment is right, the words are heard, repeated, passed on. Every prophet knows this.

Words also travel *In*. Repeated morning after morning, they go deep, plant themselves in the heart, and change us. And we become who we most want to be: makers of a better world, a world for children. We find ourselves stepping off the curb, speaking up, acting out, serving notice to government leaders:

Stop the killing of children in wars, stop making war, now.

To say the *Promise* is to speak what conscience demands.

At work in the Promise is a quiet power: empathy. The absolute love I feel for my child is the same absolute love every parent feels for their child, wherever they live, whatever language they speak. This is common ground. Love's ground. And empathy places us there. And there, together—mothers, fathers, grandparents, aunts, uncles, god parents, foster parents, honorary neighbor parents—we can say:

> *I we will not be a part of the killing*
> *of any child . . .*
> *not your child, not my child,*
> *not the enemy's child.*

To say the *Promise* is to let our love of one child become our love of every child.

The time is right. Our world has become small. Air travel, television, mass migrations, and global business have made it small. And now, the internet. A dance step posted on Tik-Tok in Tulsa is picked up overnight by young people in Jerusalem, Johannesburg, Bangkok. A germ leaked from a laboratory in rural China becomes, in days, a worldwide epidemic. A neighborhood bombed in Aleppo sends a family of five, wet and penniless and barely alive, onto the shores of Sicily. At the death of Buddhist peacemaker Thich Nhat Hanh, candles are lit on altars in Berlin, Lagos, Salt Lake City.

What religions have always taught, and science discovers, has become obvious: We are one. Our survival is mutual. Only when your child is safe is my child safe.

A Promise to Our Children is a global movement *to end the killing of children in wars.* This can happen. It begins with you and me saying the *Promise*. The words will carry, be heard, and said by others, and by groups. Reading groups, AA groups, parent groups. Civic groups will begin their meetings with the *Promise*. Congregations will end their worship services with the *Promise*. From you to me . . . to groups . . . communities . . . whole countries. A plane of connecting circles radiating out. And at each circle's center, a person committed to the *Promise*, saying it and living it.

This is how systemic change happens. The people of India sought independence from the British by a person-by-person commitment to nonviolent noncooperation with the military occupation. And what seemed impossible happened: Britain left without a single shot fired at them.

This is how the people of the Philippines ended the military dictatorship of Ferdinand Marcos. Millions of citizens, one at a time, saying, "no more," and then saying it together.

This is how the Civil Rights movement prevailed and became law in the United States. One woman, Rosa Parks, refused to sit at the back of a bus, and her example ignited the determination for justice in person-after-person. It became a bus boycott, lunch counter sit-ins, voter registration drives, and street marches. And finally, a vote in the Houses of Congress.

To say the *Promise* is to commit to systemic change through non-violent action. To say the *Promise* and live it is to serve notice to our leaders, "No to war. Any war."

The Invisible Child
WAR'S UNSPEAKABLE BARGAIN

A Fourth Telling

The three stories—Ivan's challenge to Aloysha—the child imprisoned in the basement in Omelas—the girl in the pink dress on the runway—are *imagined*, but their truth is not. The facts of that truth are told to us daily in the news: reports of bombed neighborhoods, schools, hospitals; reports of drones sending Hell Fire missiles into homes, cars, restaurants; photos of mothers and fathers digging through rubble to find the body of their child; photos of children wounded, starving, ragged, alone.

The story is from an interview with investigative reporter David Phillipps by Sabrina Tavernise titled, "How the U.S. Hid a Deadly Airstrike." It aired on The Daily, *The New York Times,* Nov 15, 2021. The following is my summary of that interview.

> *On March 18, 2019, a group of about 80 refugees gathered on the mud bank of the Euphrates river outside Baghuz, Syria. They were fleeing the U.S. bombing campaign against Islamic State fighters. Ragged and exhausted, the refugees curled up on the ground to sleep.*
>
> *Above, a U.S. drone transmitted photos of the group to a U.S. combat operations center in Al Udeid, Qatar. There, on large computer screens, Air Force personnel*

monitored the situation. They saw mostly women and children, no weapons, and no threat. Suddenly, a low flying U.S. F-15 jet appeared. It dropped a 500-pound bomb directly on the group. Then came another F-15. It dropped a 2000-pound bomb.

The Air Force watchers were stunned. When the smoke cleared, they saw that all but a few of the refugees were dead. They wondered if they had just witnessed a war crime. They sent a video of the bombing to Dean Korsak, the military lawyer responsible for reviewing combat actions involving civilians. He thought a crime might be involved and sent the report on to the head legal officer. No action was taken.

Concerned, Korsak went over his chain of command and sent the report to the Office of Special Investigations at the Department of Defense. Again, no action was taken.

Finally, Korsak hand delivered the report to the civilian Senate Armed Services Committee. They said they could do nothing because the incident was "classified."

These efforts through the military system took about two years, and no action was taken. It was then that Times reporter David Phillipps began his investigation. He discovered that the airstrike on the refugees was ordered by a secretive unit---Task Force 9, a small group of Army Delta Force commandos and Special Forces Green Berets. They worked with local militia and could, if they were in imminent danger, call in airstrikes. Phillipps found that the Task Force routinely called in airstrikes claiming "self defense," and that the March 18 bombing was just one instance of the unit's bypassing supervision.

Phillipps also found video evidence that just four days after the March 18 bombing, the military had begun a cover up. Military bulldozers arrived at the site and plowed under the bodies, the backpacks, blankets, and cups. All evidence buried. What remained was a clean stretch on a Syrian riverbank.

~

The Invisible Child is real. Boys and girls---each with a name, a mother, a father, a home, a future—sacrificed so that our comforts continue. What can we do? Something obvious and immediate: make *A Promise to Our Children*. It begins,

> *I will not be a part of the killing,*
> *of any child, no matter how lofty the reason.*

Thank You

Thank You Michael Nye for the use of the photograph of the Kurdish girl for the cover. Thank You Tim Gilman (timmyroland.com) for layout and design. Thank you Deb Hobbie and Adam Vogal, The Peace Professionals, for serving as editors. Thank you first readers for your insights and encouragement: Rod De Luca, Mitzi Jenson, and Frances Menlove. Thank you Sherry Hoesly at The Permissions Group Inc. for gaining the necessary copyright permissions. Thank you donor friends who support *Fields of Peace* and its Mission: to stop the killing of children in wars.

Credits

Epigram
A Thousand Moons, by Sebastian Barry, Viking, London, 2020, p 47

A Beginning Word
Sweeny Todd, music and lyrics by Stephen Sondheim
U.N. Convention of the Rights of the Child, 1990

First Telling
The Brothers Karamazov, by Fyodor Dostoyevsky, tranl. Pevear and Volokhonsky, North Point Presse, 1990, San Francisco, p 245

The Numbers: The ratio of combatant to civilian deaths comes from U.N. agencies, NGOs, and universities that monitor war casualties. The consensus among them, consistent for the past four decades, is that 90 percent of the people killed in modern warfare are civilians. Our sources include:

Casualties of Conflict, Department of Peace and Conflict Research, Uppsala University, 1991

Impact of Armed Conflict on Children, by Graca Machel, expert of the Secretary-General of the U.N., 1996

Human Development Report, U.N., 1998

Stanford / News Service, 1/24/2011: Report by Cynthia Haven on Richard Goldstone's comments at a symposium on "Ethics and War."

American Journal of Public Health, June, 2014

"Civilian Casualties in Modern War," *Georgia Journal of International and Comparative Law,* 8/28/2014

Body Count, Physicians for Social Responsibility, 2015

Note: The most recent reports from *Save the Children,* 2020, include:

- Five times as many children die in violent conflict zones than combatants
- 450 million children world-wide—1 in 6—live in violent conflict zones.
- 200 million children live in the world's most lethal war zones.
- An average of 25 children are killed or injured daily in violent conflict zones

Second Telling
the wind's twelve quarters, "The Ones Who Walk Away from Omelas," by Ursula K. Le Guin, Harper Perennial, New York, 1976, pp 281, 282 Copyright ©1973 by Ursula K. Le Guin. First appeared in "New Dimensions 3" in 1973, and then in THE WIND'S TWELVE QUARTERS, published by HarperCollins in 1975. Reprinted by permission of Ginger Clark Literary, LLLC

Third Telling
A Promise to Our Children, A Field Guide to Peace, by Charles P. Busch, *Fields of Peace,* p 56

A Last Word
New York Times, Daily Show, Nov 15, 2021, Sabrina Tavernise interview with reporter Dave Phillipps.

"Civilian Deaths Mounted as Secret Unit Pounded ISIS," *The New York Times*, Dec. 12, 2021, by Dave Phillipps, Eric Schmitt, Mark Mazzetti.

"National Defense and Dead Children," by peace journalist Robert C. Koehler, 2021 Chicago Tribune Content Agency, Inc.

The Invisible Child
WAR'S UNSPEAKABLE BARGAIN

Fields of Peace

Fields of Peace envisions a world in which all conflicts are solved peacefully.

Originally created in 2007 as the adult education wing of *Peace Village Inc.*—an international program teaching children how to solve conflicts through peaceful means—today Fields of Peace is an independent 501c3 nonprofit based in Oregon.

A Promise to Our Children is an initiative that envisions the daily repetition of a Promise together with transformative acts of conscience and heightened empathy for the "other," across enough geographies globally, to end the killing of children in wars.

Given the enormity and urgency of this work, Fields of Peace seeks long-term alliances with like-minded individuals and organizations to join our mission, giving voice and action to this message at home and afar. We are one world, one humanity, and must co-exist peacefully for the sake of our children and generations to come.

Our Alliances include: The War Prevention Initiative; World Beyond War; The Nuclear Age Peace Foundation, and Shanti Sahyog Center for Nonviolence, New Delhi.